BIGGEST NAMES IN MUSIC

HARRY STYLES

by Emma Huddleston

T0014729

FOCUS
READERS®
NAVIGATOR

WWW.FOCUSREADERS.COM

Focus Readers is distributed by North Star Editions:
sales@northstareditions.com | 888-417-0195

Produced for Focus Readers by Red Line Editorial.

Photographs ©: Isabel Infantes/Press Association/AP Images, cover, 1, 20–21; Charles Sykes/Invision/AP Images, 4–5, 25; David Mirzoeff/PA Wire URN:50784697/Press Association/AP Images, 7; Shutterstock Images, 8–9, 11, 14–15, 17, 18, 22; Dominic Lipinski/PA Wire URN:10317429/Press Association/AP Images, 13; Joel C Ryan/Invision/AP Images, 26; Yui Mok/PA Wire URN:24610475/Press Association/AP Images, 29

Library of Congress Cataloging-in-Publication Data
Names: Huddleston, Emma, author.
Title: Harry Styles / by Emma Huddleston.
Description: Lake Elmo, MN : Focus Readers, 2021. | Series: Biggest names in
  music | Includes index. | Audience: Grades 4-6
Identifiers: LCCN 2020013674 (print) | LCCN 2020013675 (ebook) | ISBN
  9781644936399 (hardcover) | ISBN 9781644936481 (paperback) | ISBN
  9781644936665 (pdf) | ISBN 9781644936573 (ebook)
Subjects: LCSH: Styles, Harry, 1994---Juvenile literature. |
  Singers--England--Biography--Juvenile literature. | One Direction
  (Musical group)--Juvenile literature.
Classification: LCC ML3930.S89 H84 2021 (print) | LCC ML3930.S89 (ebook) |
  DDC 782.42164092 [B]--dc23
LC record available at https://lccn.loc.gov/2020013674
LC ebook record available at https://lccn.loc.gov/2020013675

Printed in the United States of America
Mankato, MN
082020

ABOUT THE AUTHOR

Emma Huddleston lives in the Twin Cities with her husband. She enjoys writing children's books and staying active. She thinks music is an important part of life and spends some afternoons learning how to play the piano.

TABLE OF CONTENTS

CHAPTER 1

LIVE PERFORMANCE

Harry Styles stood onstage and smiled. A small audience watched him in the studio. Millions more watched on TV. He was hosting a November 2019 episode of *Saturday Night Live* (*SNL*). *SNL* is a comedy show. After greeting the audience, Styles sat at a piano. He played a few notes and told a few jokes.

Harry Styles performs on NBC's *Today* show in February 2020.

Later, Styles acted as characters in comedy **skits**. The audience enjoyed seeing his many talents. Then came the moment many people had been waiting for. Styles stepped onstage to perform his new song "Watermelon Sugar." The song was from *Fine Line*, his second **solo** album. The album would be released in December. People were excited to hear Styles's new music.

Pink lights glowed onstage. Styles's deep, clear voice rang out. Guitars and a keyboard played in the background. When Styles reached the **refrain**, a group of brass instruments joined in. Styles sounded cool and confident. He spun

Styles remains a fan favorite after more than a decade of performing.

around and did a few dance moves. The audience clapped and cheered for him.

Styles had become famous at age 16 as part of a band. Nearly 10 years later, he was proving his abilities as a solo artist. Whether he is with a band or on his own, people love seeing him perform.

CHAPTER 2

GETTING DISCOVERED

Harry Edward Styles was born on February 1, 1994. He grew up in Cheshire, England, with his parents and sister. His family listened to a lot of music. His dad often listened to Queen and the Rolling Stones. His mom often played Shania Twain and Norah Jones. These artists influenced Harry over time.

Harry had been singing for years before he gained the attention of fans.

Harry was always passionate about music. As a young teen, he and some friends started a band. They mostly sang **cover songs**. But they wrote a few originals, too. Harry was the lead singer of the band.

At age 16, Harry's life changed. His mom encouraged him to **audition** for *The X Factor.* It was a TV show and singing competition held in the United Kingdom. In early 2010, Harry entered the solo category. For his audition, he sang "Isn't She Lovely" by Stevie Wonder. Harry passed the audition and made it to the next round of the contest. But he was cut several weeks later.

Harry gained a lot of fans for his singing on *The X Factor.*

However, Harry's journey wasn't over. The judges had noticed his talent. Instead of sending Harry home, they grouped him with four other male soloists. The boys learned to sing together. They continued the competition in the group category.

Harry came up with a name for the new group: One Direction. Week after week, fans voted for One Direction. The band made it to the contest's final round. There, the boys performed "Your Song" by Elton John. The stage was dark. Then one by one, spotlights lit up

STAIRWELL DIARIES

While filming for *The X Factor*, the boys of One Direction started a video diary. They sat together in a stairwell. They talked about what was happening in their lives. They told funny stories. Then they posted the videos online. Fans loved getting to learn more about the singers. The stairwell diaries helped One Direction connect with fans. The band gained many supporters.

One Direction continued performing as a group after *The X Factor* season ended.

the five singers. The boys stood in a line onstage. They sang together. The crowd cheered loudly when they finished. The show ended in December 2010, and One Direction took third place. It was only the beginning of the band's success.

CHAPTER 3

WORLD-FAMOUS BAND

Styles dropped out of school after *The X Factor*. He chose to focus on his musical career. He became the lead singer of One Direction. Less than a year after forming, the band signed a US **record deal** in 2011. Then, in February 2012, One Direction's first **single**, "What Makes You Beautiful," came out.

After *The X Factor*, Styles had fans screaming at him wherever he went.

The upbeat pop song was a test. The band wanted to see if its music would be popular in the United States. It was. Over time, the song went platinum four times. Going platinum means selling more than one million copies.

One Direction's fame continued to grow in 2013 and 2014. Fans around the world were drawn to the band's catchy songs. In August 2013, a movie came out about the band. The movie was called *One Direction: This Is Us*.

In 2014, the band traveled for its *Where We Are* tour. The boys performed for more than 3.4 million fans worldwide. The tour made more than $290 million. It was the

"What Makes You Beautiful" was on One Direction's first album. *Up All Night* was released worldwide in 2012.

biggest music tour of the year. Then, in November 2014, One Direction released *Four.* On that album, Styles wrote the words for "Where Do Broken Hearts Go." He showed his talent as a songwriter.

The boys of One Direction didn't say when they might get back together. Fans were sad that the band might be over.

Four was the last album with all five band members. Zayn Malik chose to leave One Direction in March 2015. But Styles and the other members stayed together for one more year. They went on tour.

They released the album *Made in the A.M.* However, the band didn't last. The group announced it was taking a break in 2016. Styles believed it was the right decision. He felt worn out from touring, making music, and trying to have a normal life.

NEARLY 200 AWARDS

Styles kept very busy while in One Direction. He often felt rushed to write new music. He had to write songs while touring. But that hard work paid off. One Direction had a short but successful career. The band sold more than 7.6 million albums in the United States alone. It won nearly 200 awards. These included seven BRIT Awards and seven American Music Awards.

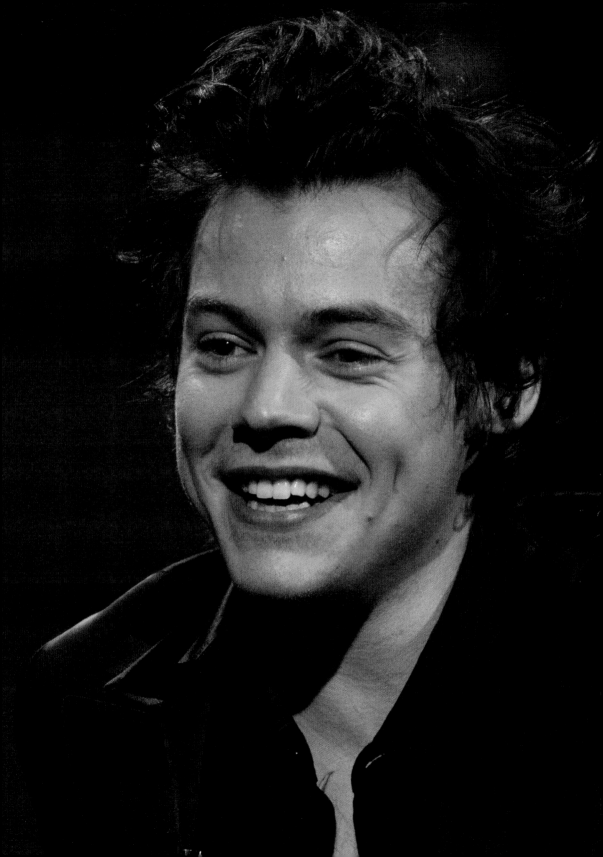

CHAPTER 4

GOING SOLO

In June 2016, Styles signed a solo record deal. He worked on his first solo album throughout the summer and fall. Fans were eager to see how his music would compare to One Direction's. In March 2017, Styles released "Sign of the Times." The song was slower and more serious than the cheery songs he used to sing.

Styles lived with his band in Jamaica as he took time to finish his first solo album, *Harry Styles*.

Styles has many musical influences, including David Bowie, the Rolling Stones, and Van Morrison.

Still, many people loved it. *Rolling Stone* magazine named it the best song of 2017.

In May, the full album came out. *Harry Styles* reached No. 1 on the charts in the United States and the United Kingdom. The album had a variety of songs on it, such as rock and pop songs. The variety showed Styles's multiple interests.

On the album, Styles aimed to be honest. He wanted to share his personality. Styles didn't have to make all his musical decisions with a group anymore. So, he wrote songs based on his own experiences. He sang about love and relationships. Styles picked those topics because he thought they were the most relatable. The album led to Styles's first solo tour. Then, he took a short break from music.

Throughout his musical career, Styles has supported various causes. For example, Styles supports **LGBTQ** rights.

Black Lives Matter is also important to him. This movement aims to build power in local communities. It also speaks out against **state violence** against black communities. Styles spreads supportive messages on social media to promote these causes.

Styles has donated to charities since early in his musical career. As members of One Direction, he and Liam Payne raised more than $800,000 for a cancer charity. On his own, Styles has raised money for more than 60 charities around the world. He has also cut his hair and donated it. The hair was made into wigs for children who needed them.

Styles is known for wearing unusual and eye-catching clothing.

In October 2019, Styles surprised fans with new music. He released "Lights Up." The song was part of his second solo album, *Fine Line*. The full album came out two months later. His popularity grew.

Styles performed his song "Falling" at the BRIT Awards in February 2020.

Styles received nominations for British Male Solo Artist and Album of the Year at the 2020 BRIT Awards. Then, he planned another tour called *Love On Tour*. It was set to start in the United States in 2021.

Styles's music ranges from boy-band pop songs to touching, slow tunes. He has made songs everyone can enjoy. And his musical career shows no signs of slowing down. Harry Styles remains one of the biggest names in music.

BEYOND MUSIC

Styles has acted in a few television shows and commercials. He acted in a movie for the first time in July 2017. The following summer, he stepped into the fashion world. He modeled for the Italian fashion company Gucci. Styles enjoys wearing bright colors. He says clothes can add more to a performance. In 2019, Styles created a fragrance with Gucci. It's called *Mémoire d'une Odeur*, which means "the memory of a scent."

HARRY STYLES

- Birth date: February 1, 1994
- Birthplace: Cheshire, England
- Family members: Anne (mother), Desmond (father), Gemma (sister)
- High school: Holmes Chapel Comprehensive School
- Major accomplishments:
  - February 2012: One Direction releases its first and most popular song, "What Makes You Beautiful."
  - April 2014: One Direction begins its *Where We Are* tour.
  - May 2017: Styles releases his first solo album, *Harry Styles*.
  - December 2019: Styles releases his second album, *Fine Line*.

The four remaining members of One Direction did their final performance as a group on *The X Factor* in 2015.

- Quote: "Of course I'm nervous. I mean, I've never done this before. . . . I'm happy I found this band and these musicians, where you can be vulnerable enough to put yourself out there. I'm still learning . . . but it's my favorite lesson."

Cameron Crowe. "Harry Styles' New Direction." *Rolling Stone*. Penske Business Media, 18 Apr. 2017. Web. 24 Feb. 2020.

FOCUS ON
HARRY STYLES

Write your answers on a separate piece of paper.

1. Write a paragraph describing how Harry Styles became famous.

2. If you were a musical artist, would you want to be a soloist or part of a group? Why?

3. When did One Direction begin taking a break?
   - **A.** 2013
   - **B.** 2016
   - **C.** 2019

4. How might taking a break help musicians?
   - **A.** It gives musicians time to relax or write new music with less pressure.
   - **B.** It helps musicians earn more money from their music.
   - **C.** It makes musicians more popular because fans notice they are on a break.

Answer key on page 32.

GLOSSARY

audition
To try out for a part in a play or musical group.

cover songs
New performances of songs that were originally written and performed by someone else.

LGBTQ
Letters that stand for lesbian, gay, bisexual, transgender, and queer.

record deal
An agreement where an artist makes an album that a company sells and promotes.

refrain
A repeated section of a song.

single
A song that is released on its own.

skits
Short plays or acts.

solo
Performing alone, not as part of a group.

state violence
When state officials such as police officers commit acts of violence against citizens of that state.

TO LEARN MORE

BOOKS

Barghoorn, Linda. *Harry Styles*. New York: Crabtree Publishing, 2018.

Gagne, Tammy. *Harry Styles*. Hallandale, FL: Mitchell Lane Publishers, 2018.

Walker, Carolina. *You Can Work in Music*. North Mankato, MN: Capstone Press, 2018.

NOTE TO EDUCATORS

Visit **www.focusreaders.com** to find lesson plans, activities, links, and other resources related to this title.

INDEX

Answer Key: **1.** Answers will vary; **2.** Answers will vary; **3.** B; **4.** A